# FROM MOVE IT TO WE DON'T TALK ANYMORE

# THE CLIFF RICHARD STORY

WRITTEN BY
THELMA SMITH

# Table of contents

# Preface

Sir Cliff Richard, known formally as Harry Rodger Webb, is an extraordinary figure in the realm of music and entertainment. Born on the 14th of October in 1940, this British artist's journey is as captivating as his voice. What sets him apart is the intriguing blend of his Indian heritage and his British and Barbadian citizenship, which adds layers of depth to his life story.

Astonishingly, Sir Cliff Richard has left an indelible mark on the music industry, having sold over 21.5 million singles in the United Kingdom alone. This staggering achievement cements his status as the third-best-selling artist in the history of the UK Singles Chart, trailing only the iconic Beatles and Elvis Presley. His early career, marked by a rebellious spirit and a musical style reminiscent of Presley and Little Richard, showcased him as a pioneering rock and roll singer.

In the late 1950s to the early 1960s, Sir Cliff Richard, along with his backing group, the Shadows, reigned supreme in the British popular music scene, preceding the meteoric rise of the Beatles. Their music resonated with a generation, and his 1958 hit single, "Move It," is celebrated as Britain's inaugural authentic rock and roll song.

Richard's artistic journey wasn't limited to music alone. In the early 1960s, he took to the silver screen, showcasing his acting prowess in films like "The Young Ones," "Summer Holiday," and "Wonderful Life." He even ventured into the world of television with his own show on the BBC, a testament to his multifaceted talents.

However, as the years passed, a remarkable transformation occurred in Richard's life and career. His deepening commitment to his Christian faith led to a gradual shift in his musical style, which became more aligned with contemporary Christian music. This transformation only added to his mystique and the multifaceted nature of his career.

With a career spanning a staggering 65 years, Sir Cliff Richard's accolades and achievements are nothing short of awe-inspiring. He amassed numerous gold and platinum discs, in addition to receiving prestigious awards like the Ivor Novello Awards and Brit Awards. His record of having more than 130 singles, albums, and EPs in the UK Top 20 stands as a testament to his enduring popularity.

Impressively, Richard boasts 67 UK top ten singles, second only to Elvis Presley. He holds a record shared only with Presley for making the UK singles charts in all six decades from the 1950s to the 2000s. His 14 UK No. 1 singles and the unique distinction of having a No. 1

single in each of five consecutive decades set him apart as a true music legend.

Sir Cliff Richard's global influence cannot be overstated. With over 250 million records sold worldwide, he stands as one of the best-selling music artists of all time. Remarkably, his popularity is a phenomenon that transcends borders. While he may not have achieved the same level of stardom in the United States, his eight US Top 40 singles, including the million-selling hits "Devil Woman" and "We Don't Talk Anymore," underline his international appeal.

Canada, too, embraced Sir Cliff Richard during the early 1960s, late 1970s, and early 1980s. His work there was met with certification of gold and platinum records. His appeal extends far beyond the UK, touching the hearts of audiences in Australia, New Zealand, South Africa, Northern Europe, and Asia. His dedicated following knows no geographic bounds.

When not gracing the stage with his music, Sir Cliff Richard divides his time between the idyllic locales of Barbados and Portugal, underscoring his well-earned reputation as a globetrotting artist. His recent relocation to New York in 2019 is yet another chapter in his ever-evolving story, demonstrating that even after six decades in the industry, he continues to be a figure of fascination and relevance.

# Early Life And Background

The early life of Cliff Richard is a tale rooted in the rich tapestry of history. Born as Harry Rodger Webb on the 14th of October in 1940, his first cries echoed through the halls of King George's Hospital, now known as KGMU Hospital, on Victoria Street in Lucknow. This city, at the time, was a part of British India, adding a unique layer of cultural and geographical significance to his origin.

Cliff Richard's parents, Rodger Oscar Webb and Dorothy Marie Dazely, embarked on a remarkable journey of their own. His father was a manager for a catering contractor, a role intricately tied to servicing the Indian Railways. In their pursuit of a better life, they traversed various parts of India, including Howrah in West Bengal.

The backdrop of history played a pivotal role in their life decisions. The violence of Direct Action Day, a tumultuous event in India's struggle for independence, acted as a catalyst for their choice to make a life-changing decision. They opted to relocate to Britain, a move that would prove to be pivotal in shaping the destiny of their son, Cliff Richard.

In the tapestry of his heritage, Cliff Richard's roots run deep. While primarily of English descent, his lineage weaves in the intriguing threads of diversity. He can trace his ancestry to one great-grandmother who was a captivating blend of Welsh and Spanish heritage. This remarkable ancestor was born of a Spanish great-great-grandmother named Emiline Joseph Rebeiro, adding a touch of exoticism to his already fascinating story.

The Webbs found their humble abode in the quaint neighbourhood of Maqbara, situated near the bustling heart of Hazratganj, the main shopping centre. In the midst of this vibrant part of Lucknow, they carved out a simple and warm family life.

Dorothy's familial ties extended into the realm of education, as her mother took on the role of the dormitory matron at the prestigious La Martiniere Girls' School. This connection to a respected educational institution would later become a part of Cliff Richard's own narrative, as he journeyed through life and embraced a path that would lead him to international fame.

Within the close-knit Webb family, Cliff Richard was not an only child. He shared his childhood and adolescence with three beloved sisters, each with her own unique name and personality. These sisters were Joan, Jacqui, and Donna, the latter of whom graced this world from 1942 until 2016, leaving behind cherished memories and a familial legacy that enriched the story of the Webb family.

The year 1948 marked a significant turning point for the Webb family. In the wake of India's newfound independence, they embarked on a transformative journey that would change the course of their lives. A three-week sea voyage aboard the SS Ranchi carried them from the shores of British India to Tilbury, Essex, England. The memories of their homeland now mingled with the promise of a new beginning in a foreign land.

This transition was more than just a change of location; it was a shift from relative affluence to a more modest life. In India, the Webbs had enjoyed the comfort of a company-supplied flat in Howrah, near the bustling city of Calcutta. This was a life of privilege and security.

However, their new life in England was quite a departure. They settled into a semi-detached house in Carshalton, a town nestled in the picturesque landscapes of north Surrey. The move signified a shift not only in their geographic location but also in their social and economic circumstances. It was a journey that would become a part of the rich tapestry of experiences that shaped the young Harry Rodger Webb, who would later rise to prominence as Cliff Richard.

Harry Webb's early education became an integral part of his formative years in England. He took his first steps on the path of knowledge at Stanley Park Juniors, a local primary school nestled in the heart of Carshalton. Here, amidst the whispers of schoolyard adventures and the rustling of leaves in the wind, young Harry's journey into the world of education began.

The year 1949 marked a significant development in the Webb family's life. Harry's father secured employment in the credit control office of Thorn Electrical Industries, leading to a change of residence. The family relocated to Waltham Cross in Hertfordshire, where Harry continued his educational pursuits at Kings Road Junior Mixed Infants School. The pages of his school days unfolded against the backdrop of this new town, with its own unique charm and character.

This period of transition saw the Webb family residing with relatives while awaiting the allocation of a three-bedroom council house. In 1950, the long-awaited move took place, and the Webbs finally found their new home at 12 Hargreaves Close in the nearby town of Cheshunt. This house would witness the growth and transformation of young Harry Rodger Webb, setting the stage for the remarkable journey that would lead to his emergence as the legendary Cliff Richard.

Harry Webb's educational journey continued to unfold as he transitioned into Cheshunt Secondary Modern School. From 1952 to 1957, he walked the halls of this institution, laying the foundation for his future. It's worth noting that the school later underwent a transformation, evolving into Riversmead School before ultimately receiving the name Bishopslea School, a testament to the evolving history of the educational institution.

A bright student, Harry was placed in the top stream, demonstrating his academic prowess and ambition. He wasn't content with the minimum requirements; instead, he chose to stay on beyond the typical leaving age, driven by a thirst for knowledge. This determination culminated in his achievement of the GCE Ordinary Level examinations, where he secured a pass in English literature, marking a significant academic milestone.

With his educational endeavours behind him, Harry embarked on a new chapter in his life. He entered the workforce as a filing clerk, donning the hat of responsibility and embracing the world of employment at Atlas Lamps. This marked the beginning of his journey towards musical stardom.

The story of Harry Webb's early career pursuits continued to unfold. In a pivotal move, he started working as a filing clerk for Atlas Lamps, embracing the world of steady employment and the responsibilities that came with it. This was the beginning of a path that would eventually lead to his musical stardom as Cliff Richard.

Interestingly, his impact on the town of Cheshunt is lasting. A development of retirement flats, aptly named Cliff Richard Court, stands as a tribute to his enduring legacy in the place where his journey began.

Harry's journey into the world of music was ignited by his burgeoning interest in skiffle, a genre that was gaining popularity at the time. His passion was fueled by his father's support when, at the age of 16, he received a guitar as a gift. The year 1957 saw the formation of the school vocal harmony group, The Quintones, showcasing his early foray into the world of music. He didn't stop there; soon, he was lending his vocals to the Dick Teague Skiffle Group, marking the initial steps of what would become a legendary music career.

# Musical Evolution 1958-1963

The period from 1958 to 1963 marked a transformative phase in the life of Harry Webb. During this time, he stepped into the spotlight and began to ascend the ladder of success and stardom. He took on the role of the lead singer in a rock and roll group known as the Drifters, a name distinct from the well-known U.S. group bearing the same title.

A pivotal moment occurred when the forward-thinking entrepreneur of the 1950s, Harry Greatorex, recognized the potential in this up-and-coming rock 'n' roll sensation. He believed that a change of name was in order to reflect the artist's newfound identity. The name "Cliff" was chosen, not only for its melodious sound but also for its evocative connotations. "Cliff" suggested the rugged, unyielding nature of a cliff face, symbolising the essence of rock and roll music.

Yet, there was one piece of the puzzle missing: the surname. It was Ian Samwell, the brilliant mind behind "Move It," one of Cliff's iconic hits, who came up with the idea of "Richard." This surname was chosen as a heartfelt tribute to Webb's musical hero, the legendary Little Richard. With this combination of names, Cliff Richard was born, a moniker that would come to define an era of music and enthral generations of fans.

Before their inaugural performance on a grand scale, set to take place at the Regal Ballroom in Ripley, Derbyshire in 1958, a defining change occurred. The group, previously known as the Drifters, officially adopted the name that would become synonymous with musical greatness: "Cliff Richard and the Drifters." The lineup consisted of four talented members: Harry Webb, who had already embraced the stage name "Cliff Richard," Ian Samwell handling the guitar, Terry Smart mastering the drums, and Norman Mitham contributing his skills on the guitar.

Interestingly, although the other three members of the original quartet didn't continue on with the later and better-known group, the Shadows, they remained instrumental in shaping Cliff Richard's journey. Ian Samwell, in particular, continued to be an essential contributor to Richard's musical repertoire, crafting songs that would become pivotal in the artist's later career.

Their remarkable talents caught the attention of Agent George Ganjou, who was fortunate enough to witness their performance in London. Impressed by their skills and charisma, he saw great potential in the group and believed in their bright future. As a result, he recommended them to Norrie Paramor for an audition, a pivotal moment that would set the stage for Cliff Richard's meteoric rise in the world of music.

Cliff Richard's debut recording session was a momentous occasion, and it was Norrie Paramor who took the helm as the producer. For this significant moment in Richard's budding career, Paramor selected the song "Schoolboy Crush," a track that had previously been recorded by American artist Bobby Helms. This was the song that would serve as Richard's first foray into the world of professional music.

However, Paramor generously allowed Richard to include one of his own compositions for the B-side of the record. This composition was none other than the iconic "Move It," a song that would go on to become a legendary classic. The creative genius behind "Move It" was Ian Samwell, a member of the Drifters, who found inspiration for the song while riding a number 715 Green Line bus on his way to a rehearsal at Richard's house. This stroke of inspiration would set the stage for one of the most celebrated songs in the history of rock and roll.

The "Move It" recording session was brought to life with the skilled musical contributions of session guitarist Ernie Shears, who took the lead on the guitar, and Frank Clark, who provided the bassline. These talented musicians helped transform a simple composition into a timeless classic, launching Cliff Richard's career into the stratosphere of stardom.

The story of why the A-side of Cliff Richard's debut single was replaced by the intended B-side is a subject of intrigue and multiple narratives. One version of the story suggests that Norrie Paramor's young daughter played a significant role. She was so enthusiastic about the B-side, "Move It," that her praise influenced the decision to switch it with the originally planned A-side.

Another account points to the influential TV producer Jack Good, who was instrumental in using Cliff Richard's act for his TV show, "Oh Boy!" It's said that Good preferred to showcase "Move It" on his television program rather than "Schoolboy Crush," and this might have contributed to the choice of which track would become the main A-side.

In the midst of these changes and developments, Cliff Richard himself expressed a sense of nervousness as he embarked on his television debut. To adapt to the expectations of this new medium, he even went as far as shaving off his sideburns, believing that this change in appearance would make him appear more original. It was a moment of excitement and trepidation, marking the beginning of his journey into the spotlight of music and entertainment.

Cliff Richard's debut single, "Move It," made a remarkable impact on the music scene, ascending to the No. 2 position on the UK Singles Chart. This early success solidified his place as a rising star in the world of music and laid the foundation for a spectacular career.

Notably, "Move It" earned high praise from none other than John Lennon, one of the iconic members of The Beatles. Lennon credited this track as being the first British rock record, underlining its historic significance in the annals of British music.

In the early days of his career, Cliff Richard was marketed as the British counterpart to the legendary Elvis Presley. This marketing approach sought to draw parallels between Richard and Elvis, emphasising their commonalities. As part of this image, Richard adopted Elvis-like clothing and hairstyle, echoing the style of previous British rockers such as Tommy Steele and Marty Wilde. This strategy aimed to capture the spirit of rock and roll and its global appeal, which was embodied by the King of Rock and his British equivalent, Cliff Richard.

Onstage, Cliff Richard projected a distinctive rock attitude that set him apart. He often struck a pose of cool detachment, rarely breaking into a smile or making direct eye contact with the audience or the camera. This aura of aloofness became a signature element of his performance style, adding a layer of intrigue to his presence.

Following the release of his debut single "Move It" in late 1958, Richard maintained the momentum with a series of follow-up singles in the early months of 1959. "High Class Baby" and "Livin' Lovin' Doll" were among these early successes, each contributing to his rising star status.

However, it was "Mean Streak" that truly stood out. This track carried the electric energy of a true rocker, characterised by its sense of speed and unbridled passion. The fiery spirit of "Mean Streak" captivated audiences and solidified Richard's reputation as a rock and roll sensation.

In addition to these electrifying rock tracks, Richard also ventured into the realm of ballads and pop. Notably, he recorded Lionel Bart's "Living Doll," showcasing his versatility as an artist. This diversity in musical styles would become a hallmark of his enduring career in the years to come.

With the release of "Living Doll," a pivotal shift occurred in Cliff Richard's musical journey. It marked the moment when the Drifters, who had previously been a part of the live performances, began to back him on record. This collaboration signalled a new chapter in Richard's discography.

"Living Doll" was his fifth record, and it held a special place in his career. Not only did it become a significant hit, but it achieved the remarkable milestone of becoming his first No. 1 single. The song's catchy melody and timeless charm resonated with audiences, propelling him to the top of the charts.

Around this period, the Drifters went through some changes in their lineup. New members, including Jet Harris, Tony Meehan, Hank Marvin, and Bruce Welch, joined the group. These changes in personnel played a key role in shaping the distinctive sound of Cliff Richard and the Shadows, a collaboration that would define a significant portion of Richard's career.

The trajectory of Cliff Richard and his backing group took an interesting turn due to legal complications. As "Living Doll" made its way into the American top 40, it became subject to licensing issues with the American group known as the Drifters, who shared the same name. To avoid these legal entanglements and pave the way for their American debut, the group chose to alter their name, becoming "The Shadows."

"Living Doll" was not only a musical sensation but was also featured in Richard's debut film, "Serious Charge." Interestingly, for the film, the song was arranged in a different style. Instead of a rock and roll standard, it was transformed into a country standard, highlighting the versatility and adaptability of Richard's music.

This transitional period marked a significant phase in the group's evolution, setting the stage for the Shadows to make their own indelible mark on the world of music.

The Shadows were far from a typical backing group. A notable distinction was their contractual independence from Cliff Richard, which set them apart from the usual backing musicians of the era. In an arrangement that was unusual for the time, the group did not receive royalties for their contributions to records backing Richard.

In 1959, a significant development occurred when the Shadows, who were still known as the Drifters at that time, secured an independent recording contract with EMI. This contract allowed them to create their own music, distinct from their role as Richard's backing band. During that year, they released three singles, showcasing their versatility. Two of these singles featured double-sided vocals, while the third offered an instrumental A-side and a vocal B-side. This marked the beginning of their journey as a group with a unique musical identity, distinct from their role as Cliff Richard's backing musicians.

Following their independent recording contract, the Shadows embarked on a journey that would lead them to immense success. They achieved a series of major hits, including an impressive five UK No. 1 singles. This chart-topping success solidified their status as a prominent musical act in their own right.

Interestingly, the collaboration between the Shadows and Cliff Richard didn't end with their independent career. They continued to appear and record with Richard, a partnership that yielded many of his most beloved hits. Their musical synergy was a defining element of Richard's sound.

In a remarkable testament to their popularity and influence, there were occasions when a Shadows instrumental track actually replaced one of Richard's songs at the top of the British charts.

Cliff Richard's career trajectory saw a noteworthy transformation with the release of his fifth single, "Living Doll." This track marked a departure from the high-energy rock and roll of his earlier work, ushering in a softer and more relaxed sound. It was a musical evolution that resonated with audiences.

Following "Living Doll," Richard continued to achieve major success with subsequent hits. Notable among these were the chart-topping No. 1 singles "Travellin' Light" and "I Love You." These songs, along with tracks like "A Voice in the Wilderness," which was featured in his film "Expresso Bongo," and "Theme for a Dream," solidified Richard's status as a mainstream pop entertainer.

During this period, Richard stood shoulder to shoulder with his contemporaries in the British pop music scene, including artists like Adam Faith and Billy Fury. Their collective influence was undeniable, contributing to a vibrant and dynamic era in British music.

Throughout the early 1960s, Richard's string of hits consistently ranked in the top five on the charts, a testament to his enduring appeal and the evolution of his music to a softer, more melodic sound that resonated with a broader audience.

In 1961, a special and memorable event unfolded in honour of Cliff Richard's 21st birthday. EMI Records took the initiative to organise a grand celebration at its London headquarters, situated in Manchester Square. Leading the festivities was none other than Richard's producer, Norrie Paramor, who orchestrated a momentous gathering to mark the occasion.

Photographs capturing the joyous celebrations were preserved and later incorporated into Richard's upcoming album, aptly titled "21 Today." This album served as both a musical offering and a visual keepsake of the milestone celebration, reflecting the camaraderie and the jubilant spirit of the event.

Notably, despite the recent departure of Tony Meehan from the Shadows, he joined in the birthday festivities. It's worth mentioning that Meehan had very recently left the Shadows, and he would soon be succeeded by Brian Bennett in the group. This era of transition and evolution continued to shape the musical landscape of Cliff Richard and the Shadows.

In the live performances of Cliff Richard and the Shadows, there was a well-established pattern. The Shadows typically took the stage first, closing the first half of the show with a 30-minute set that showcased their own musical prowess. Then, they seamlessly transitioned to backing Cliff Richard during his show-closing 45-minute performance. This dynamic collaboration between the Shadows and Richard became a defining aspect of their live shows.

One noteworthy example of this arrangement can be found in the retrospective CD album release titled "Live at the ABC Kingston 1962." This album captures the essence of their live performances during this period, demonstrating the synergy and musical excellence of the group.

However, there were changes on the horizon. Tony Meehan and Jet Harris, two key members of the Shadows, departed from the group in 1961 and 1962, respectively. They each went on to achieve chart successes as solo artists for Decca.

To fill the vacancies left by Meehan and Harris, the Shadows introduced new members to their lineup. Bass players Brian Locking (1962–63) and then John Rostill (1963–68) joined the group, contributing their talents to the band's signature sound. Brian Bennett, who had previously played with the Shadows, returned to the group as the permanent drummer, solidifying the lineup for this iconic instrumental group.

In the early years of his career, Cliff Richard's music extended to a diverse range of styles and arrangements. This was particularly evident on album and EP releases, where he explored the realm of ballads. These ballads featured Richard backed by the Norrie Paramor Orchestra, with Tony Meehan initially serving as the session drummer and later being succeeded by Brian Bennett.

One of the earliest instances of Richard releasing a single without the Shadows was "When the Girl in Your Arms Is the Girl in Your Heart" in 1961. This marked a departure from his more rock and roll-oriented sound and showcased his versatility as an artist. Following this, he continued to release one or two ballads per year. Notable examples included his covers of songs like "It's All in the Game" in 1963 and "Constantly" in 1964, the latter being a revival of a popular Italian hit.

A significant turn came in 1965 when Cliff Richard engaged in recording sessions in Nashville, Tennessee, under the direction of Billy Sherrill. These sessions proved highly successful, resulting in chart-topping hits such as "The Minute You're Gone" and "Wind Me Up (Let Me Go)." The former claimed the No. 1 position on the UK singles chart, while the latter reached No. 2. These ballads and country-infused tracks highlighted Richard's ability to excel in a wide range of musical styles, further enriching his discography.

Cliff Richard and the Shadows, despite their immense popularity in the United Kingdom and other parts of the world, faced challenges in achieving star status in the United States. Their journey in the U.S. market was marked by a series of obstacles.

In 1960, they embarked on a tour of the United States, where they were met with a positive reception. Their live performances resonated with American audiences, showcasing their musical talents and charisma.

However, their attempts to establish a long-term foothold in the American music scene were hindered by various factors. One significant challenge was the lack of consistent and robust support from American record labels. The group experienced a revolving door of record labels in the U.S., which posed difficulties in terms of distribution and promotion.

Despite these hurdles, Cliff Richard managed to secure a few chart records in the United States, including the aforementioned "It's All in the Game," which was released on Epic Records. This achievement was facilitated by a renewed partnership between the worldwide Columbia labels, following the end of Philips' distribution deal with CBS. While they enjoyed moments of recognition, they were unable to achieve the kind of star status in the United States that they had attained in other parts of the world.

The Shadows' journey in the United States was marked by moments that might have been frustrating for the group. One notable example was their hit instrumental track "Apache," which climbed to No. 2 in the U.S. However, the version that achieved this success was a cover by Danish guitarist Jorgen Ingmann, and it closely mirrored the original worldwide hit by the Shadows. This situation could understandably have been a source of chagrin for the group.

In an attempt to break through in the American market, Cliff Richard and the Shadows appeared on The Ed Sullivan Show, a program that played a crucial role in propelling the Beatles to fame in the U.S. Despite their appearances on this influential show, their efforts did not result in sustained success in North America. It was a challenging and somewhat frustrating chapter in their journey, given their immense popularity in other parts of the world.

Cliff Richard and the Shadows made a significant impact in the world of cinema, with appearances in six feature films. Their filmography included a debut in the 1959 movie "Serious Charge," but it was their roles in films like "The Young Ones," "Summer Holiday," "Wonderful Life," and "Finders Keepers" that truly left a mark.

These films, often collectively referred to as the "Cliff Richard musicals," created a unique genre of their own. They were characterised by their musical performances and showcased the talents of both Richard and the Shadows. The combination of catchy songs and engaging storylines made these films a special treat for audiences.

Their cinematic endeavours had a profound impact, and Cliff Richard's popularity as a cinema attraction in Britain soared. In 1962 and 1963, he claimed the No. 1 position at the cinema box office, surpassing even the popularity of the iconic James Bond, a testament to the enduring appeal and entertainment value of the "Cliff Richard musicals."

"The Young Ones" was not only a successful film but also the source of one of Cliff Richard's biggest-selling singles in the United Kingdom. The title song of the film became a massive hit, selling over one million copies in the UK. This track resonated with audiences and became an iconic part of Richard's discography.

Interestingly, the title and concept of the irreverent 1980s TV sitcom "The Young Ones" were inspired by Cliff Richard's 1962 film. This television series, known for its unique humour and unconventional characters, borrowed its name from the film, reflecting the enduring cultural influence of "The Young Ones."

In mid-1963, Cliff Richard and the Shadows embarked on an exciting season in Blackpool, a popular destination for entertainment. During this period, Richard had his portrait created by the talented artist Victor Heyfron, a testament to his status as a beloved figure in British entertainment.

# Cliff Richard's Surprising Encounter with 'Honky Tonk Angel'

The emergence of the Beatles and the Mersey sound in 1963 and 1964 had a notable impact on the music landscape, and Cliff Richard, like many other established rock acts in Britain, felt the effects of this seismic shift in popular music. Although his career remained resilient, he faced a changing musical landscape.

During the 1960s, Cliff Richard continued to be a popular and chart-topping artist, maintaining his presence and releasing hit songs. However, it's fair to say that his level of dominance was not quite as high as it had been in the earlier years of his career. The British music scene was evolving, and the cultural influence of the Beatles and other emerging bands was undeniable.

Nonetheless, Richard's ability to adapt and remain relevant in changing circumstances was a testament to his enduring talent and appeal. His contributions to the music industry continued throughout this era, with a career that extended well beyond the initial wave of rock and roll.

Cliff Richard faced challenges in establishing a significant presence in the U.S. market, especially during the era of the British Invasion. While some British acts found tremendous success in the United States as part of this musical movement, Richard was not considered a prominent figure in the British Invasion.

Despite releasing four songs that made their way to the Hot 100 chart in the United States, including the top 25 hit "It's All in the Game" between August 1963 and August 1964, Richard struggled to gain recognition among the American public. His impact in the U.S. was relatively limited, and he did not experience the same level of awareness and success as some of his British counterparts during this time.

This disparity in recognition between his global popularity and his status in the American market was a notable aspect of his career during this period.

Richard's religious journey has been a significant aspect of his life and career. Although he was baptised as an Anglican in his early years, he did not actively practise the faith during that period. However, in 1964, there was a pivotal change in his life when he became an active Christian. His faith became a central and guiding aspect of his personal and professional life.

Publicly standing up as a Christian had a profound impact on his career. Initially, Richard grappled with the notion that he should quit rock 'n' roll. He felt that he could no longer continue in the same manner as the rocker who had been labelled a "crude exhibitionist" and deemed "too sexy for TV." This marked a period of reflection and transformation in his career as he reconciled his faith with his music and public image.

This decision to align his music career with his Christian faith ultimately led to a significant shift in his musical style and image, reflecting a more mature and spiritual approach to his work. It was a defining moment in his life and a testament to the depth of his religious convictions.

Cliff Richard's initial intention was to "reform his ways" and pursue a career as a teacher, a path he considered in light of his newfound Christian faith. However, his Christian friends offered advice that led him in a different direction. They encouraged him not to abandon his career solely because he had become an active Christian.

As a result of this guidance, Richard chose not to step away from his career in music. Instead, he re-emerged with a renewed perspective, embracing both his Christian faith and his musical pursuits. He began performing with Christian groups and recorded material that reflected his faith and spiritual journey.

This period marked a significant transition in his career, as he integrated his Christian beliefs into his work. It allowed him to explore a unique fusion of music and faith that resonated with both his long-time fans and those who appreciated the spiritual dimension of his music.

Cliff Richard continued to record secular songs with the Shadows, maintaining a dual musical career. However, he increasingly devoted a significant portion of his time to Christian work and activities. This included appearances with the Billy Graham crusades, a prominent and influential Christian evangelical movement.

As time progressed, Richard found a way to balance his deep Christian faith with his music career. This balance allowed him to remain one of the most popular and enduring singers in Britain while also becoming one of the country's most well-known and respected Christian figures. His ability to integrate his faith and his music endeared him to a diverse audience and solidified his status as a versatile and influential artist.

Cliff Richard's remarkable string of chart successes in the UK deserves special mention. From 1960's "A Voice in the Wilderness" to 1965's "The Minute You're Gone," he achieved an incredible feat with 23 consecutive top-ten hits in the UK. To this day, this remains a record number of consecutive top-ten hits for a male artist in the UK.

Despite some changes in his career and the evolving music landscape, Richard continued to enjoy international success. In 1967, his song "The Day I Met Marie" reached No. 10 in the UK Singles Chart and No. 5 in the Australian charts, indicating his enduring appeal and ability to connect with audiences worldwide. His impact in the music industry remained strong, reflecting both his musical talent and enduring popularity.

In 1967, Cliff Richard expanded his artistic pursuits beyond music by taking on an acting role in the film "Two a Penny." The film was released by Billy Graham's World Wide Pictures, showcasing Richard's versatility as an artist. In "Two a Penny," he played the character Jamie Hopkins, a young man who becomes entangled in drug dealing and undergoes a period of self-reflection after his girlfriend's change in attitude. This marked a significant step in Richard's acting career, demonstrating his ability to tackle complex roles and themes.

During this time, he also released a live album titled "Cliff in Japan" in 1967. This album captured his live performances and added to his extensive discography, showcasing his enduring popularity as a live performer. His creative endeavours continued to span music and film, further enriching his career.

In 1968, Cliff Richard represented the United Kingdom in the Eurovision Song Contest, performing the song "Congratulations." This upbeat and memorable song was written and composed by Bill Martin and Phil Coulter. It was a highly anticipated moment in the contest.

Despite the excitement and the catchy tune, Cliff Richard's "Congratulations" narrowly missed victory. It lost by just one point to Spain's entry, "La La La." This was an incredibly close result, and according to John Kennedy O'Connor's "The Eurovision Song Contest—The Official History," it was the closest result seen in the contest up to that point.

The intensity of the competition and the anxiety of the voting process took a toll on Richard. In an effort to manage his nerves during the tense moments of the voting, he famously locked himself in a restroom. This moment in Eurovision history remains a notable and memorable part of Richard's career.

In May 2008, a Reuters news report raised intriguing claims regarding the Eurovision Song Contest held in 1968. The report suggested that the voting in the competition had been manipulated by the Spanish dictator Francisco Franco to secure a win for Spain's entry. The motivation behind this alleged manipulation was to ensure that Spain could host the contest the following year in 1969.

According to the report, Spanish TVE television executives were said to have engaged in practices such as offering to purchase programs from other countries in exchange for votes. Additionally, there were claims of contracting unknown artists as part of an effort to influence the voting in favour of the Spanish entry.

These allegations added an intriguing historical layer to the 1968 Eurovision Song Contest and raised questions about the extent to which politics and external factors might have influenced the outcome of the competition during that time.

The claims of manipulation in the 1968 Eurovision Song Contest, which were brought to light in 2008, garnered significant attention in the media. The story received wide coverage and even became a main story on UK's Channel 4 News on May 7, 2008. Jon Snow, a prominent journalist, conducted an interview with author and historian John Kennedy O'Connor to delve into the matter and its implications.

However, it was later determined that these allegations were, in fact, untrue. The story had originated from a widely repeated rumour instigated by TVE, the Spanish television network. The intrigue and speculation surrounding the contest's voting process were dispelled by these findings.

Despite the controversy, Cliff Richard's song "Congratulations" remained a resounding success throughout Europe and Australia. It reached No. 1 on the charts in April 1968, further highlighting the enduring appeal of the song and Richard's musical talent.

Following the split of the Shadows in 1968, Cliff Richard's musical career continued to evolve. In the

1970s, he ventured into various artistic endeavours. He took part in several television shows and even had his own show titled "It's Cliff Richard," which ran from 1970 to 1976. This show featured appearances by notable figures such as Olivia Newton-John, Hank Marvin, and Una Stubbs. It also included a segment known as "A Song for Europe."

Richard's presence on television in the early 1970s was substantial. He began the year 1970 with a live appearance on the BBC's "Pop Go The Sixties," a review of the music scene from the previous decade. This show was broadcast across Britain and Europe on December 31, 1969, providing audiences with a nostalgic look back at the music of the 1960s.

Cliff Richard's television and music career in the early 1970s featured several notable moments and collaborations. In 1972, he made a short BBC television comedy film titled "The Case," which featured appearances from comedians and marked a special milestone in his career. Notably, this project included his first-ever duets with a woman, and his partner in these duets was Olivia Newton-John.

This creative period also led to the release of a double live album titled "Cliff Live in Japan 1972." The album showcased Richard's live performances and included collaborations with Olivia Newton-John, further highlighting their musical partnership.

In 1973, Cliff Richard took on his final acting role on the silver screen up to that point. He starred in the film "Take Me High," marking the conclusion of his film career as of that year. These endeavours expanded his artistic repertoire and contributed to the richness of his career.

Cliff Richard's career in the early 1970s was indeed marked by a series of significant moments and artistic collaborations. His involvement in the 1972 BBC television comedy film "The Case" represented a unique milestone in his career. This project not only featured appearances from comedians but also marked his first-ever duets with a female artist, with Olivia Newton-John being his partner in these memorable performances.

During this creative period, Richard also released the double live album "Cliff Live in Japan 1972." The album not only captured the energy of his live performances but also showcased his collaboration with Olivia Newton-John, underlining the strength of their musical partnership.

In 1973, Cliff Richard took on his final acting role on the silver screen, as of that year, with his appearance in the film "Take Me High." These diverse endeavours expanded his artistic horizons and contributed to the depth and diversity of his career.

In 1973, Cliff Richard took on the role of singing the British entry in the Eurovision Song Contest with the song "Power to All Our Friends." The song secured a respectable third place in the competition, closely trailing behind Luxembourg's "Tu Te Reconnaîtras" and Spain's "Eres Tú." To manage the anxiety and nerves associated with this high-profile performance, Richard resorted to taking Valium. In fact, his manager had quite a task waking him for the performance due to the calming effects of the medication.

Richard's association with the Eurovision Song Contest extended beyond his performance. He also played a role in hosting the BBC's qualifying heat for the Eurovision Song Contest, known as "A Song for Europe," in 1970, 1971, and 1972. These contributions were part of his involvement with the BBC TV variety series. Additionally, he presented the Eurovision Song Contest Previews for the BBC in 1971 and 1972, further solidifying his connection to this prestigious international music event.

In 1975, Cliff Richard released a single titled "Honky Tonk Angel," which was produced by Hank Marvin and John Farrar. However, at the time of its release, Richard was unaware of the song's connotations and hidden meanings. As soon as he was informed that "honky-tonk angel" was a term in southern U.S. slang used to refer to a prostitute, he was taken aback and horrified.

In response to this revelation, Cliff Richard immediately ordered EMI to withdraw the single from circulation and chose not to promote it, despite having already created a music video for the song. EMI complied with his request, even though the single was expected to sell well. As a result, only about 1,000 copies of the single on vinyl are known to exist, and it remains a unique and somewhat rare piece in his discography.

# Prolific Career and Enduring Legacy

In 1976, a pivotal decision was made to repackage Cliff Richard's image and style, aiming to position him as a rock artist. Bruce Welch played a significant role in relaunching Richard's career during this period and took on the role of producer for the landmark album "I'm Nearly Famous." This album featured several notable tracks, including the guitar-driven and somewhat controversial song "Devil Woman." "Devil Woman" went on to become Richard's first true hit in the United States, expanding his international success. The album also included the emotive ballad "Miss You Nights," showcasing Richard's versatility.

The release of "I'm Nearly Famous" was met with positive critical acclaim. In a review published in Melody Maker, Geoff Brown heralded it as the renaissance of Cliff Richard's career, marking a significant turning point in his musical journey.

Cliff Richard's return to the rock music scene was met with excitement from his fans, many of whom had been devoted followers since the early days of British rock. This revival represented a resurgence of a performer who had been integral to the British rock and roll scene from its very beginnings.

The enthusiasm for this new direction extended beyond his fan base and reached prominent figures in the music industry. Renowned musicians like Jimmy Page, Eric Clapton, and Elton John were often spotted wearing "I'm Nearly Famous" badges, symbolising their support and appreciation for Richard's return to heavier rock music. This renewed energy and enthusiasm surrounding his work were a testament to his enduring influence and appeal in the world of music.

Cliff Richard's artistic journey was marked by a multifaceted approach to his music. Despite his successful return to rock and pop music, he continued to release albums that featured contemporary Christian music content in parallel. An example of this is the 1978 album "Small Corners," which included the single "Yes He Lives."

On December 31, 1976, Richard was part of the celebration of British pop music for Queen Elizabeth II's impending Silver Jubilee. He performed his latest single, "Hey, Mr. Dream Maker," during this event, showcasing his ability to connect with diverse musical genres and audiences while staying true to his Christian beliefs and values. This dual approach allowed him to maintain a presence in both the mainstream music scene and the contemporary Christian music community.

In 1979, Cliff Richard reunited with producer Bruce Welch to create the pop hit single "We Don't Talk Anymore." The song, written and composed by Alan

Tarney, achieved remarkable success, reaching No. 1 in the UK and No. 7 in the United States. Notably, Bryan Ferry contributed hummed backing vocals to the track.

This record-breaking song held a unique place in Richard's career. It made him the first artist to reach the top 40 of the Hot 100 chart in the 1980s while having also accomplished this feat in each of the three previous decades. Due to the song's popularity, it was appended to the end of his latest album, "Rock 'n' Roll Juvenile." In the United States, the album was renamed "We Don't Talk Anymore" for its release, emphasising the impact and significance of this iconic track.

"We Don't Talk Anymore" marked a triumphant return for Cliff Richard, as it not only topped the UK singles chart but also became his biggest-selling single globally, selling nearly five million copies worldwide. This success was particularly significant as it had been over a decade since he had last achieved a No. 1 hit on the UK singles chart.

In addition to his musical accomplishments, in 1979, Cliff Richard had the honour of performing alongside the talented Kate Bush at the London Symphony Orchestra's 75th-anniversary celebration at the prestigious Royal Albert Hall. This event showcased his enduring presence in the music industry and his ability to collaborate with other notable artists on prestigious stages.

The late 1970s and early 1980s brought about a period of renewed success for Cliff Richard in the United States. Following the breakthrough of "Devil Woman" in 1976, "We Don't Talk Anymore" in 1979 marked the beginning of this extended success.

In 1980, "Carrie" broke into the US top 40, and it was followed by the hit "Dreamin'," which reached No. 10 on the charts. Richard's duet with Olivia Newton-John, "Suddenly," from the film Xanadu, peaked at No. 20, showcasing the strength of his collaboration with other artists. This success continued with "A Little in Love" reaching No. 17 and "Daddy's Home" hitting No. 23 in 1981.

In a remarkable turn of events, after many years of limited success in the United States, three of Cliff Richard's singles charted simultaneously on the last Hot 100 of 1980, namely "A Little in Love," "Dreamin'," and "Suddenly." Notably, the music videos for "We Don't Talk Anymore," "A Little in Love," and "Dreamin'" held the distinction of being among the first videos played on MTV upon the network's launch in 1981. This period marked a significant resurgence of Richard's popularity in the US music scene.

In the United Kingdom, "Carrie" achieved a No. 4 position on the charts, while "Dreaming'" reached No. 8. A retrospective review of "Carrie" by AllMusic journalist Dave Thompson offered high praise, describing it as "an enthrallingly atmospheric number" and highlighting it as one of the most electrifying recordings in Cliff Richard's career.

In 1980, Cliff Richard took a significant step by officially changing his name from Harry Rodger Webb to Cliff Richard through a deed poll. This marked a personal and professional transition for the artist. Additionally, during the same period, he was honoured with the award of Officer of the Order of the British Empire (OBE) by Queen Elizabeth II. This recognition was a testament to his remarkable contributions to music and charity, underscoring his role as an iconic figure in British culture.

In 1981, Cliff Richard continued to enjoy success with the single "Wired for Sound," which reached No. 4 in the UK. This song also became his biggest hit in Australia since the early 1960s, showcasing his enduring international appeal. To conclude the year, "Daddy's Home" climbed to No. 2 on the UK singles chart.

During this period, Richard experienced a remarkable resurgence in his career, particularly on the singles chart, where he was enjoying his most consistent period of top twenty hits since the mid-1960s. He was also achieving a string of top ten albums, further solidifying his status as a prolific and enduring artist. These albums included "I'm No Hero," "Wired for Sound," "Now You See Me, Now You Don't," a live album recorded with the Royal Philharmonic Orchestra titled "Dressed for the Occasion," and "Silver," which marked his 25th year in show business in 1983. Cliff Richard's continued success during this period underlined his status as a respected and influential figure in the music industry.

In 1986, Cliff Richard achieved another No. 1 hit by collaborating with The Young Ones to re-record his classic hit "Living Doll" for the charity Comic Relief. This special recording not only featured the song but also included comedic dialogue between Richard and The Young Ones, adding a unique and entertaining twist to the track. This collaboration showcased Richard's enduring popularity and willingness to contribute to charitable causes.

During the same year, Richard took on a unique role in the West End, portraying a rock musician tasked with defending Earth in a trial set in the Andromeda Galaxy. This creative venture was part of the multimedia Dave Clark musical "Time."

In 1985 and 1986, Richard released three singles from the concept album recorded for "Time." These songs included "She's So Beautiful," which reached No. 17 in the UK, "It's in Every One of Us," and "Born To Rock 'n Roll." This period demonstrated Richard's versatility and ongoing creative contributions to the music scene.

In August 1986, Cliff Richard found himself in a harrowing situation when he was involved in a five-car crash on the M4 motorway in West London during torrential rain. Unfortunately, his car was severely damaged in the incident, and Richard sustained an injury to his back. However, it's fortunate that the injury was not more serious. Despite the accident, he displayed remarkable resilience and dedication to his craft.

Even though he was not seriously hurt, the accident was certainly a traumatic experience. Remarkably, Richard went on to perform that same night in the musical "Time." After the show, he expressed gratitude for his safety, acknowledging that his seatbelt had played a crucial role in preventing more severe consequences. His commitment to his performance and the show under such circumstances reflects his professionalism and dedication to his craft.

In October 1986, Cliff Richard achieved success with "All I Ask of You," a duet he recorded with Sarah Brightman from Andrew Lloyd Webber's musical adaptation of "The Phantom of the Opera." This collaboration reached No. 3 on the UK singles chart, highlighting Richard's ability to adapt to various musical genres and continue to produce chart-topping hits.

The year 1987 brought the release of Richard's album "Always Guaranteed," which went on to become his best-selling album of all-new material. This album included two top-10 hit singles, "My Pretty One" and "Some People," reaffirming his enduring popularity and ability to resonate with audiences. This period marked another successful chapter in Cliff Richard's illustrious career.

In 1988, Cliff Richard marked his thirtieth year in music with a remarkable achievement in the UK. He secured the coveted Christmas No. 1 single with "Mistletoe and Wine," an enchanting holiday song that captured the festive spirit. Simultaneously, he dominated the charts with his compilation album "Private Collection," which compiled his most significant hits from the period of 1979 to 1988.

"Mistletoe and Wine" was Richard's 99th UK single, and it occupied the top spot on the chart for an impressive four weeks. It became the best-selling UK single of 1988, with a remarkable 750,000 copies sold. The album "Private Collection" achieved quadruple platinum status, marking a significant milestone in Richard's career as it became his first album to be certified multi-platinum by the BPI, especially since they introduced multi-platinum awards in February 1987. These successes reaffirmed Richard's enduring popularity and ability to connect with his audience, even after three decades in the music industry.

Cliff Richard reached a monumental milestone in May 1989 when he released his 100th single, titled "The Best of Me." This achievement solidified his status as the first British artist to accomplish such a feat. The single climbed to No. 2 on the UK singles chart, underlining his ongoing success and enduring appeal.

"The Best of Me" also served as the lead single for Richard's album "Stronger," which achieved a place in the UK top ten. The album's release was accompanied by several other successful singles, including "I Just Don't Have the Heart" (UK No. 3), "Lean On You" (No. 17), and "Stronger Than That" (No. 14). Remarkably, this album became Richard's first studio album to produce four UK top twenty hits, highlighting his continued relevance and popularity in the music industry.

In 1989, Cliff Richard received the prestigious "Outstanding Contribution award" at the Brit Awards, a recognition of his significant impact on the music industry. This award underscored his enduring influence and remarkable career.

Additionally, in June of that year, Richard staged an unforgettable event at London's Wembley Stadium, aptly titled "The Event." Over the course of two nights, he entertained a combined audience of 144,000 people, showcasing his immense popularity and ability to captivate audiences.

On June 30, 1990, Richard participated in a massive charity concert at England's Knebworth Park. The concert, which featured an all-star line-up including Paul McCartney, Phil Collins, Elton John, and Tears for Fears, attracted an estimated 120,000 people. This event, broadcast worldwide, aimed to raise funds for disabled children and young musicians and successfully collected $10.5 million for these noble causes. Cliff Richard's participation in such charitable endeavours reflected his commitment to making a positive impact beyond the realm of music.

In 1990, a live album titled "From a Distance: The Event" was released, featuring highlights from the previous year's memorable "The Event" show. This album included two live tracks that were released as singles, namely "Silhouettes" (reaching No. 10 in the UK) and "From a Distance" (achieving No. 11 on the charts). It captured the energy and magic of the live performances, allowing fans to relive the experience.

Furthermore, Cliff Richard's Christmas single "Saviour's Day" proved to be a tremendous success, marking his 13th No. 1 single in the UK and his 100th top 40 hit. The album that contained this festive hit reached No. 3 on the charts during the Christmas season and was certified double platinum by the BPI, underscoring Richard's enduring appeal and his ability to capture the holiday spirit in his music.

In 1991, following the success of his Christmas singles, Cliff Richard released his first Christmas album titled "Together with Cliff Richard." His effort to secure the UK Christmas No. 1 spot with the single "We Should Be Together" was not as successful, reaching No. 10 on the charts.

The year 1992 brought the release of "I Still Believe in You" (reaching No. 7), which served as his Christmas single. In 1993, Richard made a significant return with his first new music studio album in over three years. His ability to maintain a consistent presence on the music scene and connect with his audience was evident through his various releases during this period.

In 1993, Cliff Richard made a remarkable return with his studio album "The Album," which debuted at No. 1 on the UK album chart. The album featured several singles, including "Peace in Our Time" (No. 8), "Human Work of Art" (No. 24), and "Healing Love" (No. 19), released in time for Christmas. This period marked another successful chapter in Richard's enduring career.

In 1994, a compilation album titled "The Hit List" was released. While maintaining his musical career, Richard was also working on bringing the musical "Heathcliff" to the stage, showcasing his versatility in both music and performance.

Cliff Richard's sustained success in the late 1970s through the early 1980s, followed by another impressive period in the late 1980s and early 1990s, solidified his position as a prominent and beloved music artist with a dedicated fan base in the UK. His collaboration with various artists including Olivia Newton-John, Elton John, Stevie Wonder, Phil Everly, Janet Jackson, Sheila Walsh, and Van Morrison showcased his versatility and enduring popularity.

Additionally, the Shadows, Richard's early backing group, had their own reunions and splits over the years. They not only recorded independently but also joined forces with Richard again on several occasions, creating musical moments cherished by fans throughout the late 1970s, 1980s, and 1989-90.

# A Musical Odyssey of Reinvention and Perseverance

In 1976, Cliff Richard's career underwent a transformation as he was repackaged as a rock artist. Bruce Welch played a pivotal role in this reinvention and produced the album "I'm Nearly Famous." This album included the successful yet somewhat controversial track "Devil Woman," known for its guitar-driven sound, and the ballad "Miss You Nights." This marked a significant turning point for Richard's career. A review in Melody Maker hailed the album as the "renaissance" of Cliff Richard, emphasising the impact of this change.

Cliff Richard's career revival as a rock artist with the release of "I'm Nearly Famous" in 1976 generated significant enthusiasm among his fans. This album marked a return to his roots in the rock genre and drew support from notable figures in the music industry, including Jimmy Page, Eric Clapton, and Elton John, who were seen wearing "I'm Nearly Famous" badges. This resurgence allowed Richard to reconnect with his rock origins and engage a new generation of fans.

Cliff Richard's career during this period exhibited a multifaceted approach. While he was making a notable comeback in the rock and pop music scene, he continued to release albums that featured contemporary Christian music content. For instance, the album "Small Corners" in 1978 included the single "Yes He Lives," reflecting his commitment to Christian themes in his music. His versatility allowed him to cater to a diverse audience with different musical interests. Additionally, his performance on the BBC's "A Jubilee of Music" in 1976 demonstrated his enduring popularity and relevance in British pop culture, especially during significant events like Queen Elizabeth II's Silver Jubilee celebration.

"We Don't Talk Anymore" marked a significant milestone in Cliff Richard's career. This hit single, produced by Bruce Welch and written by Alan Tarney, achieved No. 1 in the UK and No. 7 in the US. It also set a remarkable record for Richard as the first artist to reach the Hot 100's top 40 in the 1980s while having already achieved this in each of the three previous decades. His enduring popularity and musical talent were evident in the success of this song, and it contributed to his lasting legacy in the music industry. The song's inclusion in the album "Rock 'n' Roll Juvenile," re-titled "We Don't Talk Anymore" for the US release, further solidified his presence in the international music scene.

"We Don't Talk Anymore" brought Cliff Richard back to the top of the UK singles chart and marked a significant milestone in his career. Notably, it was his first time at the top of the UK singles chart in over a decade, underlining his enduring popularity. The song also enjoyed remarkable international success, becoming his biggest-selling single worldwide, with almost five million copies sold globally. Richard's performance with Kate Bush at the London Symphony Orchestra's 75th anniversary celebration at the Royal Albert Hall further showcased his versatility and enduring presence in the music industry.

In 1979, Cliff Richard's career took a remarkable turn with the release of "We Don't Talk Anymore." This guitar-driven pop hit, produced by Bruce Welch, marked Richard's triumphant return as a rock artist and became his first true success in the United States. It was a significant moment in his career, and fans were electrified by the revival of a performer who had been part of British rock since its early days.

The impact of "We Don't Talk Anymore" wasn't limited to the UK. This catchy song hit the top spot on the UK singles chart and climbed to No. 7 in the US, making Richard the first artist to reach the top 40 of the Hot 100 in each of three decades. With this achievement, Richard solidified his place as a veteran artist with enduring appeal.

His success didn't stop there. In the following year, 1980, "Carrie" broke into the US top 40, followed by "Dreamin'," which achieved the remarkable feat of reaching No. 10 on the charts. Richard's collaboration with Olivia Newton-John on "Suddenly," part of the film Xanadu, hit No. 20 on the charts. It was followed by "A

Little in Love" at No. 17 and "Daddy's Home" at No. 23 in 1981. This string of hits represented a comeback for Richard in the United States.

Furthermore, these successes coincided with the launch of MTV in 1981. Several of Richard's music videos, including "We Don't Talk Anymore," "A Little in Love," and "Dreamin'," were among the first to be featured on the groundbreaking music television channel. MTV's impact on music culture was immense, and Richard's presence on the channel further solidified his resurgence in the American music scene.

While making waves in the United States, Cliff Richard was also enjoying considerable success in the UK. "Carrie," released in 1980, reached the impressive position of No. 4 on the UK singles chart, becoming a fan favourite. Following closely, "Dreamin'" soared to No. 8, securing Richard's status as a formidable chart presence in his homeland.

One particular track from this era, "Carrie," has continued to receive accolades from critics. AllMusic journalist Dave Thompson hailed it as an "enthrallingly atmospheric number" and went so far as to call it "one of the most electrifying of all Cliff Richard's recordings." This critical acclaim spoke to the song's unique appeal and its lasting impact.

In 1980, there was another significant development in Richard's life. He officially changed his name by deed poll, transitioning from Harry Rodger Webb to the iconic stage name, Cliff Richard. Simultaneously, Queen Elizabeth II recognized his incredible contributions to music and charitable work by awarding him the Officer of the Order of the British Empire (OBE).

These accomplishments marked a transformative period in Richard's life and career. His switch to the new name solidified his place in music history, while the royal recognition reinforced his commitment to making a difference in the world through his music and philanthropic efforts.

The early 1980s marked a remarkable period for Cliff Richard in terms of chart-topping success. In 1981, his single "Wired for Sound" rocketed to the No. 4 spot on the UK singles chart, making waves not only in the UK but also in Australia, where it became Richard's biggest hit since the early 1960s.

As the year came to a close, another major achievement was unlocked when "Daddy's Home" reached No. 2 on the UK singles chart. This series of chart-topping hits signalled a renaissance for Richard, firmly reestablishing him as a chart presence with incredible staying power.

Richard wasn't only succeeding in the singles arena; he was also amassing a string of top ten albums. His discography included notable releases such as "I'm No Hero," "Wired for Sound," "Now You See Me, Now You Don't," and a live album recorded with the Royal

Philharmonic Orchestra titled "Dressed for the Occasion."

The year 1983 marked a monumental milestone in his career as it celebrated his 25th year in show business. The album "Silver" was released to commemorate this remarkable achievement, solidifying Cliff Richard's status as a music icon with an enduring legacy.

In 1986, Cliff Richard took on an exciting musical endeavour by teaming up with The Young Ones, known for their irreverent humour, to re-record his iconic hit "Living Doll." This unique collaboration was for the charity Comic Relief, showcasing Richard's versatility and willingness to engage in charitable efforts. The reimagined version of "Living Doll" included not only the song but also added comedy dialogue between Richard and The Young Ones, making it a delightful and unconventional musical experience.

During the same year, Richard ventured into the world of theatre and the West End. He played the role of a rock musician tasked with defending Earth in a celestial trial set in the Andromeda Galaxy in the multimedia musical "Time," directed by Dave Clark. This immersive production provided an exciting platform for Richard to showcase his talent and stage presence, transcending the boundaries of traditional music performances.

While engaged in this creative period, several Richard singles emerged, including "She's So Beautiful," which reached No. 17 on the UK charts. Additionally, songs like "It's in Every One of Us" and "Born To Rock 'n Roll" were released between 1985 and 1986, forming part of the concept album recorded for "Time." These tracks continued to reflect Richard's artistic versatility and his ability to adapt to various musical genres and projects.

In August 1986, Cliff Richard encountered a harrowing experience when he was involved in a five-car collision during torrential rain on the M4 motorway in West London. The accident resulted from another vehicle suddenly swerving and braking hard, causing extensive damage to Richard's car, rendering it a write-off. Although the accident caused him to sustain injuries to his back, thankfully, they were not severe.

Despite the ordeal, Richard demonstrated his remarkable dedication to his craft. Following the accident, the police arranged for a cab to transport him from the accident scene. This allowed him to fulfil his commitment and perform that very night in the musical "Time," where he played a crucial role. His resolute spirit and determination to carry on with the show were evident in his post-performance statement, where he expressed gratitude for his survival and credited his seatbelt with preventing him from being ejected through the car's windscreen. This incident showcased his remarkable professionalism and fortitude as a performer.

In October 1986, Cliff Richard collaborated with the talented Sarah Brightman on a duet titled "All I Ask of You." This enchanting song was from Andrew Lloyd Webber's renowned musical adaptation of "The Phantom of the Opera." The duo's performance resonated with the public, propelling the song to the No. 3 position on the UK singles chart.

The following year, in 1987, Richard unveiled his album "Always Guaranteed." This album marked a significant milestone in his career, becoming his best-selling album featuring entirely new material. It contained two remarkable hit singles, "My Pretty One" and "Some People," both of which achieved top-10 status on the charts. Richard's enduring popularity and ability to connect with audiences were evident in the success of this album and its accompanying singles.

In a triumphant culmination of his remarkable thirty-year musical journey, Cliff Richard celebrated Christmas in 1988 with a UK No. 1 single titled "Mistletoe and Wine." This heartwarming holiday song captured the festive spirit of the season, resonating with listeners and earning the top position on the charts. "Mistletoe and Wine" held its reign as the No. 1 single for an impressive four weeks. It became not only a Christmas anthem but also the best-selling UK single of 1988, with a remarkable 750,000 copies sold.

Simultaneously, Richard achieved a rare feat by topping not only the singles chart but also the album and video charts. His compilation album "Private Collection" summarised his biggest hits from 1979 to 1988. This collection resonated with fans, underscoring Richard's enduring appeal and influence in the music industry.

The success of "Mistletoe and Wine" and "Private Collection" marked a milestone in Richard's career, not only in terms of the music he produced but also in his ongoing connection with fans. The compilation album was certified quadruple platinum by the British Phonographic Industry (BPI), making it Richard's first release to attain multi-platinum status since the introduction of multi-platinum awards by the BPI in February 1987. It was a testament to the enduring popularity and impact of this iconic artist.

Cliff Richard continued to make history as he released his 100th single, "The Best of Me," in May 1989. This remarkable achievement established him as the first British artist to reach this milestone. The single struck a chord with fans, and it climbed to the impressive position of No. 2 on the UK singles chart.

"The Best of Me" served as the lead single for his album "Stronger," which saw great success. The album reached the UK top ten and further solidified Richard's position in the music industry. Notably, this album managed to accumulate four top twenty hits on the UK charts. It was an exceptional period in Richard's career, showcasing his enduring talent and his ability to connect with audiences over the years. This accomplishment was not only a testament to his musical prowess but also a testament to the unwavering support of his devoted fan base.

In 1989, Cliff Richard's illustrious career was celebrated when he received one of the most prestigious accolades in the British music industry – the "Outstanding Contribution Award" at the Brit Awards. This honour recognized his remarkable impact on the music world and his enduring influence throughout his career. It was a testament to his enduring presence in the industry, showcasing his consistent ability to create music that resonated with audiences over the years.

In June of the same year, Richard demonstrated his unwavering popularity when he performed at London's iconic Wembley Stadium for two memorable nights. Titled "The Event," these spectacular performances drew a combined audience of a staggering 144,000 people. It was a testament to Richard's ability to connect with his audience and continue to deliver captivating live shows.

Furthermore, on June 30, 1990, Richard was part of an extraordinary all-star concert line-up held at England's Knebworth Park. The star-studded event included music legends like Paul McCartney, Phil Collins, Elton John, and Tears for Fears. This concert served a noble cause, as it was organised to raise funds for charity, specifically to benefit disabled children and young musicians. The event was televised around the world and successfully raised a remarkable $10.5 million for these worthy causes, highlighting the enduring impact of Richard's music on charitable endeavours.

In 1990, fans of Cliff Richard were treated to a special live album titled "From a Distance: The Event." This album captured the magic of Richard's remarkable performances during the previous year's "The Event" show. It featured highlights from those unforgettable nights, providing listeners with an opportunity to relive the excitement and energy of the live shows. The album included two standout live tracks that were released as singles, "Silhouettes" and "From a Distance," which achieved considerable chart success, reaching No. 10 and No. 11 in the UK, respectively.

However, it was during the Christmas season that year that Cliff Richard made history once again. His Christmas single, "Saviour's Day," not only captured the festive spirit but also soared to the top of the UK singles chart, earning Richard his 13th No. 1 single in the UK. This achievement marked another significant milestone in his illustrious career, as it also became his 100th top 40 hit, a testament to his enduring popularity with audiences.

The success of "From a Distance: The Event" wasn't limited to the singles, as the album itself achieved remarkable chart success. During the Christmas period, it reached No. 3 on the album chart and was subsequently certified double platinum by the British

Phonographic Industry (BPI). This was a fitting tribute to Richard's continued impact on the music scene and his loyal fan base.

In the early 1990s, Cliff Richard continued to embrace the festive spirit by releasing his first Christmas album, "Together with Cliff Richard" in 1991. While the album undoubtedly spread holiday cheer, his attempt to clinch the UK Christmas No. 1 spot with the track "We Should Be Together" fell just short, landing at No. 10 on the charts.

In 1992, Richard introduced another Christmas single, "I Still Believe in You," which achieved success by reaching No. 7 in the UK charts. The following year, 1993, marked the release of Richard's first new music studio album in over three years, aptly titled "The Album." This album made an impressive debut by claiming the No. 1 position on the UK album chart. The album featured various tracks, including "Peace in Our Time" (No. 8) as the second lead single, followed by "Human Work of Art" (No. 24). To top off the year and celebrate the Christmas season, Richard delivered the heartwarming "Healing Love" (No. 19) as a festive single.

In 1994, Richard treated fans to a compilation album titled "The Hit List." While this retrospective collection offered a reminder of his remarkable career, behind the scenes, Richard was engaged in a different endeavour. He was working diligently on bringing the musical

"Heathcliff" to the stage, showcasing his versatility and ongoing commitment to the world of entertainment.

The late 1970s and early 1980s brought a resurgence of hit songs and albums for Cliff Richard, reestablishing a devoted and growing fan base. He continued to be a prominent and influential music artist in the country. The late 1980s and early 1990s saw yet another strong wave of success, highlighting the enduring appeal of his music.

During the 1980s, Richard collaborated with an impressive array of artists, showcasing his versatility and musical prowess. He worked with celebrated names such as Olivia Newton-John, Elton John, Stevie Wonder, Phil Everly, Janet Jackson, Sheila Walsh, and Van Morrison. These collaborations underscored his ability to connect with a wide range of fellow musicians and his continued relevance in the music industry.

Notably, during this time, the Shadows, the iconic band that had been an integral part of Richard's early career, experienced a series of reunions and splits. They had moments when they recorded independently, but also rejoined forces with Richard in 1978, 1984, and 1989-90, reinforcing their musical partnership and contributing to the ongoing success of their collective careers.

In a momentous turn of events, Cliff Richard received the esteemed title of Knight Bachelor on June 17, 1995. This honour was officially invested on October 25, 1995. Notably, this made him the very first rock star to be knighted, a testament to his significant contributions to the music industry.

In 1996, Richard's talents extended beyond the stage and recording studio. During a rain delay at Wimbledon, he took on the role of entertainer, leading the Centre Court crowd in a spirited sing-along. Wimbledon officials had called upon him to keep the audience engaged, and his performance was a memorable and heartwarming moment in the world of sports and music.

During the late 1990s, Richard joined forces with Clive Black, the former EMI UK managing director, to establish the record label "Blacknight." This marked his venture into the business side of the music industry, where he continued to make a mark and explore new avenues for his musical endeavours.

In 1998, Cliff Richard found himself in an intriguing situation that highlighted radio stations' reluctance to play his music. He released a dance remix of his upcoming single, "Can't Keep This Feeling In," using a white label and adopting the alias "Blacknight." The song was initially featured on playlists, but the true artist behind it remained a secret.

Later, when Richard's involvement was revealed, he released the same single under his own name as the lead track for his album "Real as I Wanna Be." Both the single and the album made a notable impact, achieving a respectable No. 10 position on their respective charts in the UK. This episode underscored the challenges he faced within the music industry, despite his iconic status.

In 1999, another controversy surrounding Cliff Richard emerged when EMI, the label he had been with since 1958, decided not to release his song "The Millennium Prayer," as they believed it lacked commercial potential. Undeterred, Richard took the song to an independent label called Papillon, which released it as a charity recording to benefit Children's Promise.

Surprisingly, "The Millennium Prayer" went on to top the UK chart for three weeks, becoming his fourteenth No.1 single and, as of December 2022, remains his most recent No.1 single. This unexpected success demonstrated Richard's enduring popularity and ability to connect with audiences.

In 2001, Richard released a covers album titled "Wanted," followed by "Cliff at Christmas," another album that reached the top ten. "Cliff at Christmas" was a holiday album that featured a mix of new and older recordings, including the single "Santa's List," which reached No. 5 on the charts in 2003.

For his next album project in 2004, Richard ventured to Nashville, Tennessee, and worked with a writers' conclave to select fresh songs for the album "Something's Goin' On." This album also achieved top-10 status and delivered three UK top-20 singles: "Something's Goin' On," "I Cannot Give You My Love" (featuring Barry Gibb of the Bee Gees), and "What Car." The venture into country music highlighted Richard's versatility and ability to explore new musical horizons.

On June 14, 2004, Cliff Richard reunited with the Shadows on-stage at the iconic London Palladium. The Shadows had made the decision to re-form for another tour across the UK. This reunion marked a significant moment for fans of the legendary group and Richard himself. Interestingly, this wasn't their final reunion, as they would come together once more for a farewell tour five years later in 2009, bringing more nostalgia to their loyal audiences.

In 2006, Cliff Richard released "Two's Company," an album of duets that achieved further success by reaching the top 10. The album featured newly recorded songs alongside prominent artists like Brian May, Dionne Warwick, Anne Murray, Barry Gibb, and Daniel O'Donnell. Additionally, it included previously recorded duets with renowned musicians such as Phil Everly, Elton John, and Olivia Newton-John. This album allowed Richard to collaborate with an impressive array of talents, making it a memorable addition to his discography.

The release of "Two's Company" was coordinated with the UK segment of Cliff Richard's global tour, titled "Here and Now." During this tour, he featured not only his well-known hits but also some of his lesser-known songs, offering a mix of tracks for his audience to enjoy. Some of the songs included in the setlist were "My Kinda Life," "How Did She Get Here," "Hey Mr. Dream Maker," "For Life," "A Matter of Moments," "When The Girl in Your Arms," and even a Christmas single titled "21st Century Christmas," which impressively debuted at No. 2 on the UK singles chart. This approach allowed Richard to provide his fans with a diverse musical experience during his live performances.

In November 2007, Cliff Richard released another compilation album titled "Love... The Album." This album, similar to "Two's Company," featured a combination of previously released tracks and newly recorded songs. Among the newly recorded songs were "Waiting for a Girl Like You," "When You Say Nothing at All," "All Out of Love," "If You're Not the One," and "When I Need You." One of these songs, "When I Need You," was released as a single and reached No. 38 on the charts. The album itself reached No. 13 on the chart, providing fans with a fresh collection of love-themed songs to enjoy.

# 75 Years of Music, Milestones, and Everlasting Impact

In 2008, Cliff Richard celebrated his 51st year in the music industry with the release of an eight-CD box set titled "And They Said It Wouldn't Last (My 50 Years in Music)." This extensive box set provided a comprehensive retrospective of his long and illustrious career. To mark this milestone, he also released a single titled "Thank You for a Lifetime" in September. The single, which celebrated his 50 years in pop music, resonated with his fans and quickly climbed the UK music charts, reaching an impressive No. 3 position. It was a significant moment in recognition of his enduring impact on the music industry.

In November 2008, Cliff Richard's official website made a significant announcement – Cliff and the Shadows would reunite to celebrate their 50th anniversary in the music industry. This was an exciting development for fans who had long appreciated their collaboration. Just a month later, they had a special performance at the Royal Variety Performance, marking a memorable moment in their reunion.

The year 2009 witnessed Cliff Richard and the Shadows embarking on a "Golden Anniversary concert tour of the

UK." This tour was a fitting celebration of their remarkable partnership over the years, making it a significant chapter in their shared history.

In September 2009, a much-anticipated album titled "Reunited" was released, featuring Cliff Richard and the Shadows. This album marked their first studio project in a remarkable forty years. It consisted of 28 tracks, with 25 re-recordings of their earlier work and three "new" tracks, which included the single "Singing the Blues," along with renditions of Eddie Cochran's "C'mon Everybody" and the Frankie Ford hit "Sea Cruise." The album made its debut at No. 6 on the UK charts during its opening week and reached a peak position of No. 4.

Their reunion tour was not limited to the UK and extended into Europe in 2010, allowing fans across the continent to enjoy their music. Furthermore, in June 2009, reports emerged that Cliff Richard was planning to return to Sound Kitchen Studios in Nashville to record a new album. This time, he was focusing on original recordings of jazz songs and had an ambitious schedule to record fourteen tracks in a week. This showcased Richard's continued commitment to exploring diverse musical genres and creating new material.

In 2010, Cliff Richard continued to share his music on significant occasions. He performed "Congratulations" at the 70th birthday celebrations of Queen Margrethe II in Denmark on April 13th, marking another memorable moment in his extensive career.

On October 14, 2010, Richard celebrated his own 70th birthday in style by hosting a series of six concerts at the iconic Royal Albert Hall in London. These concerts were a gift to his fans on this momentous occasion. To complement these performances, he released a new album, "Bold as Brass," which featured his interpretations of swing standards. This album was released on October 11th, allowing his fans to enjoy more of his music.

The official celebration for Richard's 70th birthday took place on October 23, 2010. This joyous event was attended by esteemed guests, including Cilla Black, Elaine Paige, and Daniel O'Donnell, creating a fitting tribute to his long and illustrious career.

In late October 2010, Cliff Richard embarked on a musical journey to participate in the German Night of the Proms concerts in Belgium. His performance was met with enthusiasm and surprise by the 20,000 fans at Sportpaleis Antwerp when he made an unexpected appearance. Richard treated the audience to the iconic hit "We Don't Talk Anymore," earning an enthusiastic reaction from the crowd.

Following this exciting concert, he continued his musical journey by touring 12 cities in Germany throughout November and December 2010 as the headline act during the Night of the Proms concerts. These concerts, totaling 18 in all, were a massive success, attracting over 300,000 fans who enjoyed Richard's performances, including his hits and songs from the "Bold As Brass" album.

In November 2010, he reached another milestone by achieving his third consecutive UK No. 1 music DVD in three years with the DVD release of "Bold as Brass." This success underscored his enduring popularity with fans.

October 2011 marked the release of Cliff Richard's "Soulicious" album, a remarkable musical endeavour that showcased his incredible vocal talents alongside American soul singers. This album featured a range of soulful duets with iconic artists such as Percy Sledge, Ashford and Simpson, Roberta Flack, Freda Payne, and Candi Staton. The project was produced by the renowned Lamont Dozier, adding a touch of soulful magic to the collection.

To celebrate the release, Richard embarked on a short UK arena tour, giving fans the opportunity to experience the magic of "Soulicious" live. The album's success was evident as it became Richard's 41st top-10 hit album in the UK, demonstrating his enduring appeal and versatility as a performer.

In June 2012, Cliff Richard had the privilege of participating in the Diamond Jubilee concert held outside Buckingham Palace, celebrating the remarkable 60-year reign of Queen Elizabeth II. The event brought together a stellar lineup of performers to mark this historic occasion.

Another momentous experience for Richard took place on June 30, 2012, when he played a special role in the lead-up to the 2012 Summer Olympics in London. He joined the torch relay for the Olympics, carrying the iconic Olympic torch from Derby to Birmingham. This experience held such significance for him that he considered it one of his top-10 memories, a testament to the importance of the event and its impact on his life.

Cliff Richard played a notable role in a campaign aimed at extending copyright protection for sound recordings in the UK. The objective was to extend the copyright duration from 50 to 95 years, providing musicians with the opportunity to receive royalties for a longer period. However, the initial campaign was not successful, resulting in the expiration of copyright for many of Richard's early recordings in 2008.

A renewed effort in 2013 led to a more favourable outcome. Copyright protection for sound recordings was extended to 70 years after their first publication to the public, covering works that were still under copyright at that time. This means that Richard's recordings made between 1958 and 1962 are now out of copyright in the UK, while those from 1963 will remain in copyright until 2034.

In November 2013, Richard marked a significant milestone by releasing the 100th album of his illustrious career, titled "The Fabulous Rock 'n' Roll Songbook." At that point, he had amassed an impressive discography, including 47 studio albums, 35 compilations, 11 live albums, and 7 film soundtracks.

In June 2014, Cliff Richard had an exciting concert scheduled as the opening act for Morrissey at the Barclays Center in New York, with its 19,000-capacity venue. Morrissey expressed his honour and excitement about having Richard as part of the event. However, just days before the concert, on 16 June 2014, Morrissey had to cancel the performance due to collapsing with an "acute fever." In response, Richard decided to stage a free show for his fans in New York on the same night the originally scheduled concert was meant to take place. It was a generous gesture to make up for the disappointment caused by the cancellation.

To celebrate his 75th birthday in October 2015, Cliff Richard embarked on a tour, gracing the stage in seven cities across the UK. This included an impressive six-night run at the iconic Royal Albert Hall in London, a venue where he had performed on over 100 occasions throughout his remarkable career. The tour garnered praise, with a positive review from Dave Simpson, The Guardian's rock music critic, highlighting the enduring appeal and talent of Cliff Richard.

In August 2018, Cliff Richard thrilled his fans with the announcement of a new album titled "Rise Up." This album featured fresh and original material. The album's first single, "Rise Up," was released in vinyl format and achieved an impressive No. 1 ranking on the UK Vinyl Singles Chart in October 2018. Richard also collaborated with the Welsh singer Bonnie Tyler on a duet titled "Taking Control," which was part of her 2019 studio album, "Between the Earth and the Stars."

Continuing to share his music with the world, Richard released another album titled "Music... The Air That I Breathe" in 2020. His contributions to music were further celebrated when he performed his 1963 hit "Summer Holiday" at the 2022 Wimbledon Championships, as part of the Centenary Celebration. This was yet another milestone in his enduring career.

# Challenges and Unique Position in the Music Industry

Cliff Richard has not been shy about expressing his concerns regarding the music industry's lack of commercial support. He highlighted this issue during an appearance on The Alan Titchmarsh Show on ITV in December 2007. Richard emphasised that not only emerging bands but also well-established artists like himself depended on airplay for promotion and album sales. His criticism shed light on the challenges that artists face in an industry that sometimes appears to favour newer talent over seasoned performers.

Cliff Richard has observed that radio stations in the 1980s were more supportive and played his records, which contributed to maintaining his media presence and sales. He expressed his disappointment with certain music documentaries, like "I'm in a Rock 'n' Roll Band!," for failing to acknowledge his significant contributions to the history of British music, along with his band, the Shadows. This raises concerns about the underrepresentation of his legacy in such narratives.

Richard faced instances of radio personalities taking positions against him in the late 1990s and early 2000s. In 1998, Chris Evans, who hosted the breakfast show on

Virgin Radio at the time, publicly declared he wouldn't play Cliff Richard's records, citing his age as a reason. Similarly, in June 2004, Tony Blackburn, a British disc jockey, was suspended from his radio position at Classic Gold Digital for defying station policy by playing Richard's records. The station's head of programmes, Paul Baker, expressed that Richard's music did not align with their brand values. These incidents reflect some challenges Richard experienced with radio airplay and public reception during certain periods of his career.

Tony Blackburn's suspension from his radio show at Classic Gold Digital was confirmed after he read the email from the station's head of programs on air and proceeded to play two songs by Cliff Richard, contrary to the station's directive. This incident highlights the tensions that occasionally arose regarding Richard's airplay on certain radio stations.

Absolute Radio '60s made a deliberate decision to exclude Cliff Richard's records from their playlist, citing that his music didn't align with the "cool sound" they were aiming to promote, focusing instead on acts like the Beatles, the Rolling Stones, the Doors, and the Who. Cliff Richard expressed his disagreement with this decision, suggesting that they were being dishonest with themselves and the public. These instances shed light on the ongoing challenges that some established artists, like Richard, faced in getting airplay on certain radio stations.

Cliff Richard has been open about his irritation with the praise some stars receive for indulging in drug use. In 2009, he emphasised that he's proud to be considered the "most radical rock-and-roll singer Britain has ever seen" because he chose not to engage in drugs or sexual promiscuity. Richard stands by the fact that he never adopted the hedonistic lifestyle often associated with rock stars and has never had a desire to "trash a hotel room." His clean and disciplined lifestyle has been a defining feature of his career.

Cliff Richard has criticised the music industry for encouraging artists to court controversy. In November 2013, he voiced concerns about the changes in the music industry, particularly how they can harm young artists. He criticised the sexually explicit public image of singer Miley Cyrus and expressed his discomfort with singer Alice Cooper's visual imagery and mock horror in the 1970s. He also commented on the self-destructive impulse he observed in the rock band Oasis in 1997. Richard's perspective highlights his reservations about the industry's impact on artists and their behaviour.

Cliff Richard's lack of commercial support among radio stations has been a subject of discussion. Journalists like Sam Leith have noted that his strong Christian beliefs, clean-living lifestyle, and his passion for his Portuguese winery have made him somewhat of an enigma for a younger generation more accustomed to a culture of alcohol and pop music. Additionally, John Robb suggested that Richard's rebellion against the traditional rock star lifestyle by abstaining from alcohol and drugs has made him a countercultural icon, as he effectively "rebels against rebellion." This unique stance in the music industry has contributed to Richard's distinctive position in pop culture.

Cliff Richard has expressed concerns about the reception of two of his singles, "Mistletoe and Wine" and "The Millennium Prayer," which he felt generated a negative reaction. He highlighted the significance of airplay for achieving successful singles, but noted that there appeared to be an age-related bias within the radio industry. Richard suggested that this ageism might hinder the support for new songs if he were to record them in the current music climate. This raises the issue of how radio airplay can impact an artist's ability to reach a broad audience, and the challenges that artists like Richard face in a changing music industry.

Tony Parsons, an author and rock music critic, made a notable statement about Cliff Richard, suggesting that not appreciating at least some of Richard's music means not truly appreciating pop music. This emphasises Richard's significance in the pop music landscape. Additionally, Sting, a respected musician himself, praised Richard's singing abilities and described him as one of the finest British singers both technically and emotionally. These remarks highlight Richard's influence and talent in the music industry, as recognized by fellow artists and critics.

# Personal Loss, Relationships, and Changing Perspectives

Cliff Richard experienced profound personal losses during his life. His father, Rodger Webb, passed away in 1961 at the age of 56, which had a significant impact on Richard. He reflected on the fact that his father missed the best parts of his career, and they grew closer during his father's illness.

Tragically, Richard's mother, Dorothy, faced a challenging battle with Alzheimer's disease for a decade and eventually passed away in October 2007 at the age of 87. In a 2006 interview, he shared the difficulties he and his sisters encountered while caring for their mother during her illness. These personal experiences demonstrate the challenges he faced while maintaining his career.

Cliff Richard has remained a lifelong bachelor. In a three-page letter penned in October 1961 to his "first serious girlfriend," Australian dancer Delia Wicks, which was made public in April 2010 after her unfortunate passing from cancer, Richard expressed the challenges of maintaining a lasting relationship due to his career as a pop singer. He acknowledged the difficult decision he had to make and hoped it wouldn't cause too much pain. This letter sheds light on the sacrifices he felt he had to make for his career.

During the 18 months they were dating, Richard's letter to Delia Wicks revealed the complexity of their relationship. He expressed that he couldn't give up his career, as he was a pillar of support for his mother and sisters since his father's passing. Richard had a deep attachment to showbiz, stating that it ran in his veins, and he couldn't imagine life without it. His letter encouraged Wicks to find someone who could provide her the love and commitment she deserved and who was free to marry her. This letter underscores the difficult choices he made in pursuit of his career.

Delia Wicks' brother, Graham Wicks, revealed that she had been deeply affected by Richard's decision to end their relationship and had found it devastating. He described Richard as a "very pleasant man."

In the years following his breakup with Delia Wicks, when he was 22, Richard had a brief romance with actress Una Stubbs. In the 1960s, he also contemplated marriage to dancer Jackie Irving, whom he found to be incredibly beautiful and with whom he was inseparable for a period. However, Jackie Irving later married Adam Faith. Richard's personal life had its complexities and relationships that left an impact on those involved.

In his autobiography, Richard emphasised that he was not primarily driven by sexual desires. However, he did acknowledge an incident of seduction by Carol Costa, who was estranged from Jet Harris at the time.

During the 1980s, Richard contemplated proposing to Sue Barker, a former French Open tennis champion and Wimbledon semi-finalist. He admitted considering marriage but ultimately decided that he didn't love her enough to commit to spending the rest of his life with her. Richard's personal life has seen various romantic encounters and considerations over the years.

Richard and Sue Barker's relationship began in 1982, when she was 25 years old. Their romance garnered significant media attention, especially after Richard travelled to Denmark to watch her tennis match, and they were subsequently photographed together at Wimbledon. In early 1983, Richard mentioned the possibility of marriage with Barker, stating that he was enjoying their time together. However, by September 1983, he clarified that he had no immediate plans for marriage, though he expressed a desire to settle down and have a family one day. In July 1984, Barker confirmed her affection for Richard, stating that they loved each other. Their relationship had its share of media coverage and speculation.

After his romance with Sue Barker ended, Richard remained friends with her and emphasised their mutual respect for each other in 1986. He stated that this friendship was significant to him. When asked why he had never married, Richard mentioned a few "false alarms" and the significant time commitment required by marriage. He also mentioned that he was in love during the early 1970s, and Olivia Newton-John was the object of his affections. However, she was engaged to someone else at the time, and he regretfully missed his chance with her.

In 1988, a poignant family experience touched Cliff Richard's life deeply. His nephew, Philip Harrison, faced a challenging start in life, as he spent the initial four months of his existence in a children's hospital, battling serious breathing problems. This difficult ordeal was an emotional journey for the family as they watched the young child fight for his health.

As a result of this personal experience, Richard became inspired to give back. He actively participated in fundraising efforts to support the children's hospital located in East London, which had played a pivotal role in saving his nephew's life. The artist used his influence and resources to contribute to the cause, ensuring that other families could receive the vital medical care and support needed in similarly challenging circumstances.

This act of generosity and gratitude reveals a compassionate side of Cliff Richard, reflecting his commitment to helping others and his deep appreciation for the medical professionals who made a significant difference in his family's life.

While Cliff Richard has never entered into matrimony, he has seldom dwelled in solitude. For an extended period, he shared his primary residence with his manager responsible for charity work and promotional schedules, Bill Latham, along with Latham's mother, forming a close-knit household. In 1982, Richard affectionately regarded them as his "second family."

The familial atmosphere in his home was enriched further as Latham's girlfriend, Jill, joined them and became a part of this shared living arrangement in their residence in Weybridge, Surrey. It was a unique living situation that reflected Richard's strong bonds and connections with those close to him.

Bill Latham, in 1993, acknowledged the bachelor status of Cliff Richard and highlighted that his freedom had allowed him to devote himself to a range of activities with great intensity. Richard's passion for his career, unwavering faith, and his later dedication to tennis were central aspects of his life that he wholeheartedly pursued. Latham suggested that if Richard were to enter into a relationship, he would invest himself completely, and the commitments to his career, faith, and sports were the focal points that defined his life.

This insight into Richard's life portrays his dedication to various facets of his existence, emphasising the depth of his commitment and the importance of his personal relationships.

Cliff Richard has remained discreet about his close relationships, often declining to discuss them. Over the years, he has faced speculation regarding his sexual orientation, with some suggesting that he might be homosexual. However, Richard has unequivocally stated that he is not gay.

In the late 1970s, when confronted with these suggestions, Richard responded firmly, denying the rumours and expressing his discontent with the unfair criticisms and judgments made by others. He clarified that he has had girlfriends and emphasised that he values the institution of marriage. His commitment to marriage and reluctance to enter it merely to appease societal expectations or perceptions became evident in his response.

Furthermore, Richard has shared that the rumours about his sexuality, particularly those suggesting he might be homosexual, were previously very painful for him. These speculations shed light on the challenges he faced in the public eye and how he chose to address them with candour and authenticity.

Through the years, Cliff Richard has consistently addressed questions about his sexual orientation. When asked in 1992 whether he had ever considered the possibility of being gay, he replied with a resolute "No." Richard maintained that regardless of his marital status, some people would always believe what they wished to believe. He emphasised that the opinions of those close to him, such as family and friends who trusted and respected him, held far more significance than external judgments over which he had no control.

In 1996, Richard reiterated his stance, asserting that he was aware of the rumours but making it clear that he was not gay. His comments highlighted his determination to maintain his authenticity despite the speculations that surrounded him. The following year, in 1997, he championed the rights of single individuals, emphasising that those who are not married should not be treated as second-class citizens and should feel neither embarrassed or guilty about their status. Richard expressed that everyone has a unique role to play in life.

Cliff Richard's deep faith was significantly tested in 1999 when he grappled with the shocking murder of his close friend, Jill Dando, a prominent British television presenter. The loss of someone he cherished deeply shook him to his core. He candidly admitted that he felt a profound anger towards God, grappling with the inexplicable tragedy that had taken away someone as beautiful, talented, and kind-hearted as Dando.

In his tributes to Jill Dando, Richard frequently highlighted her remarkable qualities and emphasised her genuineness as a person. Her senseless murder left him bewildered and bewildered. He found it challenging to make sense of the tragic event that had unfolded.

Despite the pain and confusion, Cliff Richard attended Jill Dando's funeral in May 1999, showing his deep respect and emotional connection with his departed friend. The sombre occasion brought together friends, family, and admirers who shared their grief and memories of the beloved television presenter.

In the early 2000s, Cliff Richard formed a close and enduring friendship with John McElynn, an American who had previously worked as a missionary. They first crossed paths during a visit to New York City in 2001. Over the years, their friendship grew stronger, and their connection deepened.

In 2008, Richard revealed that John McElynn played a significant role in his life. McElynn had taken on the responsibility of managing Richard's properties, relieving the legendary singer of these burdens. Beyond the professional aspects of their relationship, John became more than just a caretaker; he became a trusted companion and a valued presence in Richard's life. This close bond provided comfort and companionship for Richard, who, even in his later years, expressed a preference for not living alone. Their enduring friendship brought joy and support to Richard's life.

Cliff Richard has been blessed with a circle of good friends who have played a significant role in preventing him from feeling lonely. These friends have provided him with companionship and someone to talk to during various stages of his life. In a 2002 interview with David Frost, Richard expressed gratitude for these close relationships.

One such enduring friendship is his connection with Gloria Hunniford, a Northern Irish broadcaster. Their friendship has spanned over four decades, a testament to the strong bond between them. During a particularly challenging time, when Hunniford's daughter Caron Keating was diagnosed with breast cancer and chose to keep her illness private, Richard was one of a select few close friends who knew about her condition. This group of trusted confidants provided support during the difficult period. When Caron Keating sadly passed away in April 2004, Richard attended her funeral in Kent and paid tribute to her by performing his song "Miss You Nights." This heartfelt gesture was a poignant display of his love and friendship for the family during their time of loss.

Cliff Richard's connection with Portugal has been a significant part of his life. In 2006, he was honoured with the title of Commander of the Order of Prince Henry (ComIH) by the Portuguese government. This prestigious order recognized Richard's extensive involvement in Portugal, both personally and professionally, spanning four decades. His contributions included investments in winemaking and the acquisition of a house in the beautiful Algarve region, where he has enjoyed spending part of his year over the years. His deep connection to the country and his significant investments were acknowledged through this special recognition.

Additionally, in the 2002 "100 Greatest Britons" list, a public vote organised by the BBC, Cliff Richard was ranked 56th. This ranking is a testament to his enduring popularity and influence as a British icon.

Cliff Richard has demonstrated a shift in his views on certain issues over the years, as detailed in his 2008 autobiography. He expressed a more open and non-judgmental stance on matters, particularly concerning same-sex marriage. Richard called on the Church of England to recognize and affirm the commitment of people in same-sex marriages. In his words, "In the end, I believe, people are going to be judged for what they are. It seems to me that commitment is the issue, and if anyone comes to me and says: 'This is my partner – we are committed to each other,' then I don't care what their sexuality is. I'm not going to judge – I'll leave that to God." This reflects a more inclusive and accepting perspective on relationships and human identity.

In 2009, there was extensive coverage in the British media about the close friendship between Cliff Richard and Cilla Black. Reports suggested that they had explored real estate options together in Miami and were frequently spotted in each other's company, whether in Barbados, Marbella, or enjoying tennis matches from the Royal Box at Wimbledon. Both artists had homes in Barbados. After Cilla Black's passing in August 2015, Richard spoke fondly of her, describing her as "incredibly gifted" and "full of heart." He expressed his deep sadness at losing a cherished friend and paid tribute to her by performing the song "Faithful One" at her funeral in Liverpool. Their friendship was marked by shared experiences and mutual admiration, creating a strong bond between the two iconic British artists.

In 2010, Cliff Richard revealed that he had officially become a non-resident of the United Kingdom and was granted citizenship by Barbados. He emphasised that while he was no longer a resident of the UK, he would always maintain his British identity and be proud of it. At that time, Richard split his time between residing in Barbados and Portugal, enjoying life in these different parts of the world. This change in residency allowed him to explore new horizons while remaining deeply connected to his British roots.

In February 2013, when asked about whether he had any regrets regarding not starting a family, Cliff Richard reflected on his life choices. He explained that his commitment to his career had been a priority for him. Richard believed that if he had been married with children, he wouldn't have been able to dedicate as much time to his music and other endeavours. He acknowledged that his three sisters had families of their own, and he enjoyed being a part of their lives. Although he believed he could have been a good father, Richard expressed contentment with the path he had chosen, which allowed him the freedom to pursue his career and maintain a strong connection with his family.

# Philanthropic Contributions and Public Stance on Scottish Independence

In 1971, Cliff Richard actively supported the Nationwide Festival of Light, a movement composed of British Christians who held concerns about the direction of the permissive society. Richard, alongside notable figures like Malcolm Muggeridge, Mary Whitehouse, and Bishop Trevor Huddleston, took part in demonstrations in London. Their purpose was to advocate for love and family values while expressing opposition to pornography and what they considered moral corruption. Muggeridge strongly criticised the media, asserting that it was predominantly controlled by individuals who favoured the ongoing moral decline and the abandonment of religious values. This movement aimed to counteract what they perceived as a negative societal trend.

The Nationwide Festival of Lights campaign took issue with the increasing prevalence of sexually explicit films. Richard was among the roughly 30,000 individuals who congregated at London's Trafalgar Square to participate in this demonstration. Their protest specifically targeted the Swedish sex education film "Language of Love," which was being screened at a nearby cinema. The movement sought to voice their concerns about what they perceived as an encroachment of explicit content into the public sphere.

Since March 1966, Richard has been dedicated to donating a minimum of one-tenth of his income to charitable causes. He has articulated that his approach to managing his finances is influenced by two key biblical principles. Firstly, he emphasises that it's the love of money, not money itself, that is the root of all evil. Secondly, he believes in being a responsible steward of the resources entrusted to him. In his view, those who have something to offer should be consistently willing to give to support important causes.

Cliff Richard's commitment to charitable work extends for over four decades. He is a dedicated supporter of Tearfund, a Christian charity that works to alleviate poverty in numerous countries worldwide. Richard has personally visited various locations, including Uganda, Bangladesh, and Brazil, to witness Tearfund's efforts in action. His belief is that combating poverty is a collective responsibility, and he strives to play a role in making a difference.

Additionally, Richard has contributed to Alzheimer's Research UK, a charity focused on dementia research. He has actively participated in raising both funds and awareness for the cause by openly discussing his mother's battle with the disease.

Cliff Richard's philanthropy extends to numerous UK charities, largely facilitated through the Cliff Richard Charitable Trust. He has made generous donations and frequently visited various establishments, including schools, churches, hospitals, and homes for children with special needs.

Additionally, Richard's passion for tennis, partly fueled by his former girlfriend Sue Barker, led to the establishment of the Cliff Richard Tennis Foundation in 1991. This charity has played a vital role in introducing tennis to thousands of primary schools across the UK, providing tennis sessions that have engaged over 200,000 children and toured the country. The foundation has since become an integral part of the charitable initiatives of the Lawn Tennis Association.

In August 2014, Cliff Richard joined a group of 200 public figures who signed a letter to The Guardian, collectively expressing their hope that Scotland would choose to remain part of the United Kingdom in the upcoming referendum on Scottish independence. This public statement reflected his support for the unity of the United Kingdom.

# Legal Battle and Victory

In August 2014, a search was conducted at Cliff Richard's apartment in Berkshire following a complaint made in the context of Operation Yewtree. This operation was initiated to investigate allegations of sexual misconduct, particularly in the aftermath of the Jimmy Savile scandal. It's important to note that Richard was not arrested during this search and vehemently denied any wrongdoing. The way the search was handled received criticism, with the BBC's coverage of the event coming under scrutiny. Lord Macdonald of River Glaven, QC, who served as the former Director of Public Prosecutions, condemned the police's actions, referring to them as "completely disreputable conduct," and expressed concerns about the legality of the search warrant.

Cliff Richard decided to cancel several public events, including a visit to the US Open tennis championships and a scheduled appearance at Canterbury Cathedral, as he did not want these occasions to be overshadowed by the false allegation that had been made against him. He later returned to the UK and voluntarily met with members of South Yorkshire Police, where he was interviewed. It's important to highlight that Richard was neither arrested nor criminally charged throughout this process. Subsequently, David Crompton, the chief constable of South Yorkshire Police, faced criticism for his interactions with the BBC regarding this case and publicly issued an apology to Cliff Richard.

In February 2015, South Yorkshire Police announced that the inquiry into the alleged offences had increased and would continue. Cliff Richard maintained that the allegations were "absurd and untrue" in a released statement. This development followed an independent report's conclusion that South Yorkshire Police had violated Richard's privacy by disclosing information about the property search to the BBC in August 2014. A review conducted by former chief constable Andy Trotter found that the police force had breached guidelines on protecting the identity of those under investigation, and the handling of the search had damaged their reputation. The BBC's knowledge of the search reportedly originated from within Operation Yewtree, although David Crompton, the chief constable of South Yorkshire Police, could not confirm its precise source.

In May 2016, South Yorkshire Police forwarded a file of evidence to the Crown Prosecution Service (CPS). The CPS then reviewed the "evidence relating to claims of non-recent sexual offences dating between 1958 and 1983 made by four men." After the review, the CPS determined that there was "insufficient evidence" to charge Cliff Richard with an offence, and no further legal action would be taken against him. In response, Richard expressed his relief, stating that he was "obviously thrilled that the vile accusations and the resulting investigation have finally been brought to a close."

Cliff Richard expressed his frustration at being named by the media despite not being charged, feeling as if he had been "hung out like live bait." South Yorkshire Police later issued a wholehearted apology to Richard after the investigation was dropped. Richard noted that while his reputation might not be fully vindicated, as the CPS policy was to state there was "insufficient" evidence, he questioned how there could be evidence for something that never happened. During the 22-month police investigation, it was revealed that a man in his forties was arrested in connection with a plot to blackmail Richard. This individual had contacted Richard's aides and threatened to spread "false stories" unless he received a sum of money.

The BBC issued a public apology to Cliff Richard on 21 June 2016, acknowledging the distress caused by their controversial broadcast. Later, on 27 September 2016, the Crown Prosecution Service confirmed that their decision not to prosecute Richard over allegations of historical sex offences had been upheld. This review came in response to applications by two of his accusers, and it reaffirmed that the decision not to charge Richard was the correct one.

In October 2016, it was reported that Cliff Richard was suing the BBC and South Yorkshire Police. Legal papers were filed at the High Court in London on 6 October 2016. South Yorkshire Police subsequently agreed to pay Richard £400,000 after settling a claim he brought against the force.

On 12 April 2018, the case against the BBC opened in the High Court. Reports suggested that Cliff Richard was seeking "very substantial" damages. On 13 April, Richard gave evidence for more than an hour, during which he described the television coverage as "shocking and upsetting." His written statement was made available online by his lawyers, Simkins LLP.

On 18 July 2018, Cliff Richard won his High Court case against the BBC and was awarded £210,000 in damages. The BBC announced on 15 August 2018 that they would not appeal against the judgement and repeated their apology for the distress Richard had been through. The Guardian estimated that the BBC's costs for legal fees and damages had reached £1.9 million after losing the case.

## Pioneering British Rock and Roll Icon

Cliff Richard's 1958 hit "Move It" is often credited as the first genuine British rock and roll record, setting the stage for the emergence of the Beatles and the Merseybeat music scene. John Lennon himself reportedly praised Richard, stating that prior to Cliff and the Shadows, there wasn't much in British music worth listening to. Cliff Richard's successful career in both performing and recording has spanned over six decades, making him a significant and enduring figure in the UK's music industry.

# Conclusion

Cliff Richard's remarkable journey through the decades has left an indelible mark on the landscape of British music. From his groundbreaking 1958 hit "Move It," often considered the first genuine British rock and roll record, to his enduring success and contributions over six decades, Richard's impact on the UK's music industry is undeniable.

His career has been a testament to resilience and adaptability, transcending generations and musical trends. Richard's collaborations with the Shadows, his exploration of diverse genres, and his commitment to reinvention have allowed him to remain relevant and celebrated. His influence on subsequent artists, notably acknowledged by John Lennon, paved the way for the emergence of the Beatles and the iconic Merseybeat music scene, shaping the course of British music.

Richard's life extends beyond his music, encompassing philanthropy, faith, and his role in supporting charitable causes. He has consistently dedicated a portion of his income to various charities, championing important initiatives such as Tearfund and Alzheimer's Research UK. His unwavering support of these organisations reflects a deep commitment to giving back and making a positive impact on the world.

Throughout his life, Richard has navigated personal challenges, maintained strong friendships, and handled the scrutiny of the public eye with grace. His candid responses to questions about his personal life and his enduring commitment to his chosen path, regardless of speculation or criticism, reveal a man of authenticity and character.

In sum, Cliff Richard's legacy is one of pioneering British rock and roll, charitable endeavours, and a unique presence in the music industry. He remains an iconic figure who has not only withstood the test of time but has also influenced the very fabric of British music, leaving an indomitable mark on the hearts and ears of music enthusiasts across the generations. As a singer, philanthropist, and cultural figure, Cliff Richard's contributions continue to resound, making him an enduring and influential force in the world of music.